Piccolo **Book of Jokes**

D0619471

Piccolo
Book of Jokes

Margaret Gossett

text illustrations by Karen Heywood

 Piccolo Pan Books

The author's thanks to Peter Pauper Press
for their kind permission to include in this book several
limericks from their delightful collection entitled
The World's Best Limericks

First published 1960 by Dobson Books Ltd
This revised edition published 1972 by
Pan Books Ltd, Cavaye Place, London SW10 9PG
14th printing 1981
ISBN 0 330 23216 9
© Franklin Watts Inc 1954
New material and revisions © Dobson Books Ltd 1960
Set, printed and bound in Great Britain by
Cox & Wyman Ltd, Reading

CONTENTS

STINGEROOS

Towards the end of a long day's drive over winding roads in the Welsh hills, a motorist was stopped by a policeman.

'I'll have to report you for driving without rear lights,' the constable said.

The motorist stepped out of his car and gave a cry of despair.

'It's not as bad as all that,' said the policeman.

The tourist replied, 'I'm not worried about the lights. But where's my trailer?'

Two big tortoises and a little one came into a café and ordered three banana splits. While they were waiting to be served they noticed it had started to rain.

'We ought to have our umbrella,' said one of the big tortoises, and the other big one agreed. They decided that the little tortoise should go home and get the umbrella. He did not want to go because he was afraid the two big tortoises would eat his banana split. But they promised not to, and finally the little tortoise started off.

A week passed, then two weeks. At the end of the

third week one of the big tortoises said, 'Oh, come on, let's eat his banana split.'

'Okay, let's,' said the other.

'If you do, I won't go for that umbrella,' screamed the little tortoise, sticking his head out from under the counter at the other end of the café.

Johnny called up the stairs, 'Mum, I tore a big hole in the seat of my trousers.'

'Take them off and leave them by the sewing machine,' his mother said, sighing. 'Then come and get another pair.'

Ten minutes went by, but Johnny did not come upstairs. His mother went down and saw the trousers by the sewing machine, but no sign of Johnny. Then she heard a rattling in the basement. So she called down the stairs, 'Are you running round down there without any trousers on?'

'No, madam,' a deep male voice answered. 'I'm just reading the gas-meter.'

Science teacher: Is there any difference between lightning and electricity?

Practical Peter: Yes. You don't have to pay for lightning.

Some Texas cowboys were sitting round a camp fire telling yarns. One of them said, 'I know an Indian who never forgets anything. The Devil can have my soul if I'm not telling the truth.'

That night the Devil appeared and said, 'Come along with me.'

'You can't have my soul,' the cowboy replied. 'I was telling the truth. I'll show you.'

Together they went to the Indian. 'Do you like eggs?' the Devil asked.

'Yes,' the Indian answered.

Then the cowboy and the Devil went away. Seventeen years later, the Devil heard that the cowboy had died, and he dashed off in search of the Indian.

'How!' the Devil said, greeting him Indian-fashion with his right arm raised.

'Fried,' the Indian replied.

A man selling vacuum cleaners knocked on the door of a remote farmhouse. When the farmer's wife opened it, the salesman said, 'Madam, I want to show you something you'll never forget.'

Before she could answer, he threw a bag of dirt onto her clean floor.

'Now,' he went on, 'I want to make a bargain with you. If this latest model Electrosucks vacuum cleaner doesn't pick up every bit of that dust, I'll eat it.'

'Here's a spoon,' the farmer's wife said. 'We haven't got electricity.'

Smart-alec customer (in a shoe shop): How much are your four-guinea shoes?

Smarter salesman: Two guineas a foot, sir.

The Scoutmaster was very bossy, but he did insist that

the boys should have good food at camp. One day he saw two Scouts carrying a large soup bowl. 'Get me a spoon. I want to taste that,' he ordered.

The boys started to object, but the Scoutmaster broke in, 'I don't want any arguments. Do as I say.'

The spoon was found, and he took a large mouthful. Then he spluttered angrily, 'You don't call this soup, do you!'

'No, sir,' one of the Scouts answered. 'We tried to explain. It's dishwater.'

Daddy had invited the boss and his wife for dinner, and it was Patsy's job to set the table. But when dinner-time came Patsy's mother said with surprise, 'Why didn't you give Mrs Pilkington a knife and fork, dear?'

'I didn't think I needed to,' Patsy explained. 'I heard Daddy say she always eats like a horse.'

Little Willie was on his first train journey, and he was enjoying it immensely. He ran up and down from one end of the carriage to the other, knocking over glasses and upsetting cups of tea all over the place. His parents were very much embarrassed and tried to get him to sit still.

'If you don't come here and be quiet,' his father said at last, 'I'll spank you.'

Little Willie ran up to the other end of the carriage and shouted back at the top of his voice, 'If you spank me I'll tell the ticket-collector how old I really am.'

A nice old lady on a crowded train kept asking the ticket-collector to tell her when they reached Derby. The ticket-collector promised, but he was very busy, and the train had already pulled out of Derby when he remembered the old lady. He quickly told the guard, who pulled the communication cord. The engine-driver backed the train into the station again.

The guard grabbed the old lady's luggage and told her to hurry up, as this was Derby.

'Oh, thank you, but I'm not getting off here,' she said. 'You see, I have no watch, and my daughter told me that when we reached Derby it would be time to take my pills.'

A fat man decided to spend his holiday in a camp where they specialized in making fat people thin. So he went into a sports shop to get some athletic shorts. He tried on a pair, and they fitted just right. But as the salesman was wrapping them up, the fat man said, 'I'd better take a smaller pair. I'm going to get a lot thinner where I'm going.'

'That's good,' answered the salesman, tying up the parcel. 'If you shrink as fast as these do, they'll just fit you.'

A lorry driver stopped when he saw another lorry turned over in a ditch, its load of tomatoes spilled in a great heap. A boy stood looking dismally at the mess.

'Come along, son,' the lorry driver said cheerfully. 'Let's go and get something to eat at the café. You'll feel better then, and afterwards I'll help you straighten up the lorry.'

The boy didn't want to go. 'I don't think my father would like it,' he muttered.

'Don't you worry,' the driver said, and he whisked the boy off to the café.

After they had eaten, the boy said, 'I still don't think my father's going to like this.'

'Stop worrying,' the driver said. 'Where is your father, anyway?'

'He's under those tomatoes.'

A tourist driving through Ipswich was not sure he was on the right road. He stopped his car and asked a farmer in a hay wagon, 'Which way is it to Newmarket, please?'

'Don't know,' the farmer answered.

'Well, then, which way is it to Bury St Edmunds?' the tourist asked.

'Don't know.'

In irritation the tourist snapped, 'Don't you know anything?'

'Well,' said the farmer, 'I ain't lost.'

The managing director of a big department store was inspecting the place one day. In the room where the parcels were wrapped to be sent out he saw a young man just leaning dreamily against the wall.

'How much do you get a week?' the managing director snapped.

'Ten pounds,' the young man answered.

The shop owner pulled ten pounds from his wallet, handed it over and said, 'Now get out of here!' Then he turned to the manager of the department and demanded, 'Who in the world took on that lazy loafer?'

'Nobody,' the man answered. 'He was just a messenger waiting to pick up a parcel.'

A Scoutmaster at camp had answered so many questions that he was tired out. Finally he made a rule. Anyone who asked a question that he himself couldn't answer would have to wash everybody else's mess kit after supper.

This did not silence Willy, who could ask more questions than anyone else. Immediately he said, 'When a rabbit digs its hole, why doesn't it leave a heap of earth round the entrance?'

The others shouted gleefully, 'Answer it yourself.'

'A rabbit starts digging its hole at the other end,' Willy explained.

The Scoutmaster looked at him scornfully. 'How could it get to the other end to start digging?' he said.

'You made the rule,' Willy answered. 'Give him your mess kits, boys.'

The teacher was taking her class on a nature walk. At one point Bill asked her, 'Do you know what has thirty-two legs, quills like a porcupine, a tail with a hook at the end of it, four eyes and bright yellow spots?'

'No, I don't,' the teacher answered.
'Well, there's one on your collar now.'

In the bank one day Simple Simon suddenly called out at the top of his voice, 'Did anyone drop a wad of notes with a rubber band round it?'

Several people standing in the bank answered, 'I did!'

'Well, I've just found the rubber band,' said the simpleton.

'Mummy, we've thought of a new game. We're going to pretend we're elephants at the circus. Will you help us?'

'Yes, indeed. What am I supposed to do?'

'You're the lady who feeds them peanuts.'

Dave's mother was worried about the health of her neighbour.

'Dave,' she said, 'run across the street and ask how old Mrs Brown is.'

Soon Dave was back. 'Mrs Brown was very cross,' he said. 'She told me it was none of your business how old she is.'

The vicar announced that next Sunday he would preach a special sermon, and in the meantime he wanted everyone to read the seventeenth chapter of Mark.

A week later he asked all those in the congregation who had read the seventeenth chapter of Mark to raise their hands. Almost everyone did so.

'Just as I thought,' the vicar said. 'My sermon will be

on Honesty. There are only sixteen chapters in the Book of Mark.'

Peter: My uncle disappeared when he was on a hunting trip.
Archy: What happened to him?
Peter: Dad says that something he disagreed with ate him.

Once there were three men travelling in an aeroplane.
Unfortunately, one fell out.
Fortunately, there was a haystack below him.
Unfortunately, there was a pitchfork in the haystack.
Fortunately, he missed the pitchfork.
Unfortunately, he missed the haystack.

American Sheriff: Young lady, I am bound to arrest you for going swimming in this here lake.
Young Lady: But Sheriff, you might have told me before I changed into my swimming suit.
American Sheriff: There ain't no law against *that*, miss.

Teacher: Tommy, your hands are very dirty. What would you say if I came to school with dirty hands?
Tommy: I'd be too polite to mention it.

The census-taker knocked on Miss Matilda's door. She answered all his questions until he asked her age. That she refused to tell.

'But everybody tells their age to the census-taker,' he said.

'Do you mean,' Miss Matilda said, 'that Miss Grace and Miss Irene Hill down at the corner told *their* ages?'

'Yes, indeed.'

'Well,' snapped Miss Matilda, 'I'm the same age.'

On the report the census-taker wrote, 'As old as the Hills.'

A GIGGLE OF GAGS

A little old lady broke her leg. The doctor put a plaster cast on and said she would have to wear it for several months. At last he came to take it off.

Eagerly she asked, 'Now may I climb stairs again?'

'Yes, indeed,' the doctor answered.

'My, what a relief!' the old lady sighed. 'You don't know what a job it was to shin up and down the drain-pipe.'

Father (at the breakfast table): That was some thunderstorm we had last night, wasn't it, Freddy?

Freddy: It certainly was.

Mother: Oh dear, why didn't you wake me up? You know I can't sleep when there's thunder and lightning.

Enthusiastic tourist: Whose skull is that one there?

Tired museum guide: That is the skull of Julius Caesar.

Enthusiastic tourist: Then whose skull is that small one beside it?

Tired guide: That, madam, is the skull of Julius Caesar when he was a small boy.

A woman riding along on a bus was eating peanuts. Trying to be friendly, she offered some to the woman who sat beside her.

'Goodness, no!' said the second woman. 'Peanuts are fattening.'

'What makes you think that?' asked the first.

'My dear,' exclaimed the second, 'haven't you ever seen an elephant?'

A lady walked down the street carrying a small box that had holes punched in the top.

'What's in that box?' a friend asked.

'A cat,' the lady answered.

'What for?'

'I've been dreaming about mice at night, and I'm scared of mice. The cat is to catch them.'

19

'But the mice you dream about are imaginary,' said her friend.

The lady whispered, 'So is the cat.'

Two men met one day. 'I'll bet you five pence you don't know what I've got in my hand,' said the first.

'A helicopter,' said the second.

The first one cautiously opened his fingers a tiny bit, looked in, then closed his fist tight. 'No, guess again,' he said.

'A rowing-boat?'

'Guess again.'

'A cow!'

'What colour?'

'Black. Pay me my five pence.'

'Not fair!' the first man wailed. 'You looked!'

Simple Simon took a friend driving in the mountains. After a while the friend said, 'Every time you go round one of those sharp curves, I get scared.'

'Then why don't you do what I do?' Simple Simon answered. 'Close your eyes.'

A cowboy on a dude ranch in the West watched one of the guests trying to saddle a horse. 'Pardon me,' he said politely, 'but you're putting that saddle on backwards.'

The guest was annoyed. 'What makes you so sure?' he snapped. 'You don't even know in which direction I'm going.'

Mr and Mrs Smith began taking French lessons.

'What are you doing that for?' a friend asked.

'We've just adopted a French baby,' Mrs Smith re-

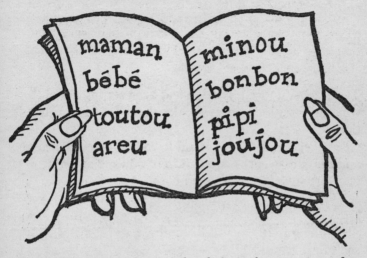

plied. 'We want to know what he's saying as soon as he learns to talk.'

Mrs Green was a careful shopper. She always asked the grocer if the eggs were fresh and the butcher if the meat was tender. One day she went into a shop to buy a packet of invisible hairpins.

'Are you sure these are invisible?' she asked before she paid for them.

'Madam,' said the shop assistant, 'I can guarantee they are. I've sold ten packets already this morning, and we've been out of them for a week.'

Simple Simon said to the doctor, 'You remember last year you told me to stay away from dampness if I wanted my rheumatism to get better?'

'I remember,' said the doctor.

'Well, it's better. Is it all right for me to take a bath now?'

The teacher noticed that Joe had been staring out of the window for a long time. She decided to catch his attention.

'Joe,' she said, 'if the world is 25,000 miles all round and eggs are twenty pence a dozen, how old am I?'

'Thirty-two,' Joe answered without hesitating.

The teacher blushed, then asked, 'How did you know?'

'Nothing to it,' Joe said. 'My big sister is sixteen and she's only half-mad.'

Friend: What are you doing?
Simple Simon: Writing a letter to my brother.
Friend: Don't try to fool me. You can't write.
Simple Simon: That doesn't make any difference. My brother can't read.

A meek little man came to the police station one day and said he wanted to make a complaint.

'I've got three big brothers,' he explained. 'We all live in one room. One of my brothers has seven cats.

Another one has five dogs, and the other has a goat. The smell in there is terrible, and I want you to do something about it.'

'Hasn't your room got any windows?' the policeman asked.

'Yes, of course it has,' the meek little man answered.

'Then open them,' was the policeman's advice.

The little man looked hurt and confused. 'And lose all my pigeons?' he said.

Simple Simon got a job nailing boards on the side of a house. Another simpleton came along and asked him why he was throwing half the nails away.

'Because the heads are on the wrong ends,' answered Simple Simon.

'You nit-wit,' said his friend. 'Those nails are for the other side of the house.'

As a policeman was walking along High Street late one night he saw a man on his hands and knees.

'Lost something?' the copper asked.

'Yes, I dropped five pence in Maple Street,' the man answered.

'If you dropped five pence in Maple Street,' said the copper, 'why are you looking for it in High Street?'

'Because,' said the man, 'there's more light here.'

Simple Simon went into a shop to buy a pillowslip.
    'What size?' asked the saleswoman.

    'I don't know,' said the simpleton. 'But I wear a size 6 hat.'

Man (to porter): When does the next westbound train arrive?
Porter: 3 PM.
Man: When will the next train be going east?
Porter: 4 PM.
Man: What about the train going north?
Porter: It arrives at 6 PM.
Man: When does the next southbound train arrive?
Porter: That left two hours ago.
Man: Well, I should think it's safe to cross the tracks now.

An estate agent was trying to interest a man and wife in renting a certain house. He finished his description of its good points by saying, 'It's only a stone's throw from the bus stop.'

'Let's take it,' the man said to his wife. 'There would always be something to do in the evening. We've never had a place before where we could throw stones at buses.'

First goon: Did you mark that place where the fishing is good?
Second goon: Yes, I put an X on the side of the boat.
First goon: That's silly. What if we should take another boat next time?

A bank had just been robbed. The police were out in full force.

'I can't understand how those bank raiders got away,' said the puzzled Chief Constable. 'Were all the exits guarded?'

'Yes, sir,' said a member of the force. 'They must have gone out by the entrance.'

A man came into a café and ordered a strawberry parfait in a long, tall glass. When it came, he carefully spooned off the whipped cream and rubbed it in his hair. Then he tossed the ice-cream behind the counter and eagerly ate up the glass. Finally he threw the stem of the glass over his shoulder.

Another customer, who had been watching the performance, tapped his arm. 'My good man,' he said, 'what *are* you thinking of?'

'I'll tell you,' was the answer. 'Whipped cream is good for the hair. I can't stand ice-cream. It's too cold. But I just love glass.'

'Of course, of course! But my good man,' said the other, 'don't you realize that the stem is the best part?'

A twittery old lady said to the assistant in a department store, 'I want to buy enough wool to knit my dog a sweater.'

'How big is he?' asked the saleswoman.

The old lady was flustered and found it hard to describe the size of the dog exactly.

'Perhaps you'd better bring him in, so that I can see how big he is. Then I can tell you exactly how much wool to get.'

'Oh, no!' said the old lady. 'It's supposed to be a surprise for him.'

Thief: Will you give your money or shall I shoot you?
Simple Simon: Shoot me. I need the money for my old age.

Simple Simon decided to walk home.

'Why don't you take the bus?' asked his friend.

'Because my mother will make me take it back.'

The new teacher was taking the class for the first time. 'In other words,' she said, 'you cannot get eggs unless you have hens.'

'Dad can,' Fred interrupted her in a cheerful voice. The teacher was a little ruffled, but she decided to ask Fred to explain. Fred did. 'Dad keeps ducks.'

PUN FUN AND WORD TROUBLE

A lady went into a shop and asked, 'May I try on that dress in the window?'

'Well—' said the assistant doubtfully. 'Don't you think it would be better to use the fitting-room?'

English teacher: Today we are going to do definitions. When you define something you tell what it is. Now, Thomas, will you define 'unaware'?

Thomas: It's the last thing I take off at night.

Dan: My grandfather had a wooden leg.

Ann: Well, my grandmother had a cedar chest.

The teacher went to call at Susie's house. 'I'd like to see your mother,' she said when Susie opened the door.

'She ain't here,' Susie answered.

'Why, Susie, where's your grammar!' the teacher said.

'She ain't here neither,' said Susie.

A woman dashed into a hardware shop and asked to be served at once. 'Give me a mouse-trap quickly, please,' she said. 'I've got to catch a train.'

'Sorry,' answered the assistant. 'We haven't got any as big as that.'

Then there was the fellow who heard a good joke and was going to take it home, but he decided that was carrying a joke too far.

Question: When is an operation funny?
Answer: When it leaves the patient in stitches.

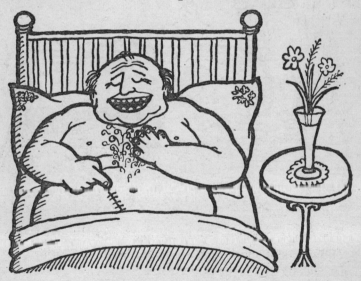

Did you hear about the chap who fell into the lens-grinding machine and made a spectacle of himself?

Lucy: Is it correct to say that you water your horse?
Mother: Yes, dear.
Lucy: Then I'm going out to milk the cat.

Question: Why is Sunday the strongest day?
Answer: Because all the others are *week*days.

A log in the forest said proudly, 'I feel fine! I slept like a human being last night.'

A local newspaper recently printed a story in which the following statement appeared: 'Mr Michael Moriarty is a new defective in the police force.'

Next week, to correct the error, the paper announced: 'Mr Michael Moriarty is a detective in the police farce.'

Question: Why did Simple Simon take hay to bed with him?
Answer: Because he wanted to feed his nightmare.

Science teacher: What family does the walrus belong to?
Alfred: Don't ask me. No family in our district has got one.

Question: What animal eats the least?
Answer: The moth. It just eats holes.

The tablecloth said to the table, 'Don't move. I've got you covered.'

Jones: Why were all your chickens out in your front garden yesterday?
Brown: They heard that men were coming here to lay a pavement, and they wanted to see how it was done.

An explorer came home with pictures of himself riding across the desert.

'Oh!' said a visitor. 'How did you ever get down off that camel?'

'I didn't,' the explorer answered.

'But you must have.'

'No, indeed. I got down off a duck.'

Johnny: I fell over twenty feet last night.
Grandmother: Oh, my! Weren't you hurt?
Johnny: No, I was just trying to get to my seat in the pictures.

Town boy: Look at that bunch of cows.
Country boy: Not 'bunch' – herd.
Town boy: Heard what?
Country boy: Herd of cows.
Town boy: Of course I've heard of cows.
Country boy: No – a cow herd.
Town boy: Why should I care what a cow heard? I've got no secrets from a cow.

'Where did I come from?' asked the baby ear of corn.
'The stalk brought you,' answered its mother.

Little Audrey just laughed and laughed as the cow slipped and fell on the ice. She knew it wasn't any use crying over spilled milk.

The busy teacher asked Charles why he had been absent.

'I had a stomach ache,' Charles answered. 'My mother said I had acid indigestion.'

'Then stop drinking acid,' the teacher snapped.

Question: Why did Simple Simon put corn in his shoes?
Answer: Because of his pigeon toes.

To avoid that run-down feeling – look both ways before crossing the street.

Teacher: What pine has the sharpest needles?
Smart Alec: The porcupine.

Two flies were sitting on Robinson Crusoe's knee.
'Goodbye now,' said one of them. 'I'll see you on Friday.'

'Will you join me in a ginger-beer?'
'Sorry. Those glasses are too narrow.'

A man was out walking in the woods one day when he came across a very odd-looking creature. It seemed to be half squirrel and half mouse. He ran home as fast as he could, picked up the phone, dialled a number, then waited and waited. Impatient at last, he called the operator and demanded, 'Why can't I get the zoo?'

'Sorry, sir,' said the operator. 'Lion's out of order.'

When can you be said to have four hands?
When you double your fists.

There was a new clerk at the Poste Restante window in the post office. One day when he was busy, a man came to the window and boomed, 'Any letters for Mike Howe?'

The clerk went on working. The man repeated the question even louder.

Without looking up, the clerk answered, 'Not for your cow, or your horse either.'

Smart Alec: I know something that's bigger when it's upside down.
Friend: What?
Smart Alec: The number 6.

First boy: My teacher shouted at me because I didn't know where the Pyramids were.
Second boy: Next time remember where you put things.

Bill: What did the bald man say when he received a comb for his birthday?

Jill: I don't know. What did he say?

Bill: Thanks very much, I'll never part with it.

Teacher: In what part of the world are people most ignorant?

Johnny: London.

Teacher: Nonsense! What makes you say that?

Johnny: My geography book says that's where the population is most dense.

The cowboy was trying to sell a dude an old horse. But for once the dude insisted on taking a ride first. When he came back, the horse was pretty well out of breath.

The cowboy started to talk fast. 'Notice what a fine coat this hoss has—'

'Never mind his coat,' said the dude. 'I don't like his pants.'

Boy (at the Fair): Who's in charge of the nuts?
Stall owner: Just a minute and I'll take care of you.

Jack: Have you ever studied a blotter?
Mac: No. Why?
Jack: It's very absorbing.

Joe: What do you sell?
Bob: Salt.
Joe: I'm a salt-seller, too.
Bob: Shake.

Sam: I've been hunting with my dad. We brought back four rabbits and a potfer.
Tim: What's a potfer?
Sam: To cook the rabbits in.

Foreign Visitor: You English must grow awfully large.
Native: Why do you think that?
Foreign Visitor: I read in one of your papers about a woman who lost five hundred pounds.

Will Harrison had to fill up one of the many forms that are a feature of life today. There was a large crowd of people, all filling up forms, and the clerk in charge was rushed.

'Fill this up,' he said, handing a piece of paper to Will. 'Put your last name first and your first name last.'

Will did not hear clearly and he asked for instructions again.

'Fill it out the way I told you – backwards,' answered the clerk.

Will shook his head, but he thought the clerk ought to know his business. He wrote his name this way on the dotted line: nosirraH lliW.

'Why did Percival leave his job?'
  'Illness.'
  'Anything serious?'
  'Yes. The boss got sick of him.'

James staggered into the room and slumped into the nearest chair. He said: 'I had the toughest time of my life. First, I got angina pectoris and then arterio uolor osis. Just as I was recovering from these, I got tuberculosis, double pneumonia and phthisis. Then they gave me hypodermics. Appendicitis was followed by tonsillectomy. These gave way to aphasian and hypertrophic cirrhosis. I completely lost my memory for a while. I know I had diabetes and acute indigestion, besides gastritis, rheumatism, lumbago and neuritis.

'I don't know how I pulled through. It was the hardest spelling test I've ever had.'

'Dad, is it correct to say that a road-sweeper sweeps roads?'

'Yes, son.'

'And a cake-mixer mixes cakes?'

'Yes, son.'

'And a weight-lifter lifts weights?'

'Yes, son.'

'Then does a shoplifter lift shops?'

Two Boy Scouts were hiking through the woods. Suddenly one stopped and sighed sadly.

'What's the matter?' asked his friend.

'Nothing,' replied the first. 'But I do wish we had a book of etiquette with us.'

The second Scout was puzzled. 'Why?' he asked.

'Because I think we took the wrong fork.'

Ray: Did you hear the one about the bed?

May: No.

Ray: No wonder, it hasn't been made up yet.

One Sunday neither of Tommy's parents could take him to church. When he got home his mother asked him what the sermon was about.

'The vicar said, "Don't worry, you'll get your scarf",' Tommy told her.

Mother, suspecting that Tommy had gone fishing – or was at least telling a fishy story – telephoned the vicar. But she found that her son had, indeed, gone to church. The subject of the sermon was 'Fear not, thy Comforter cometh.'

The fishmonger in my street swears this is true. One day a customer walked into his shop with a sad look on his face, a fishing rod in one hand and an empty creel in the other. He pointed to a lot of beautiful trout. 'I'll take five of these,' he said. 'But throw them to me.'

'Why should I throw them?' asked the fishmonger.

'I may be a poor fisherman,' answered the customer, 'but nobody can call me a liar. I want to be able to say I caught five trout.'

My uncle is a butcher. He's six feet tall and wears size 12 shoes. What does he weigh?

Answer: Meat, silly.

IT DEPENDS ON HOW YOU LOOK AT THINGS

Three slightly deaf old ladies met on a street corner.
'Windy, isn't it?' said one.

'No, it's Thursday,' said the second.

'So am I,' said the third. 'Let's all go and have a cup of tea.'

Question: Which travels more slowly – heat or cold?
Answer: Cold – you can catch cold easily.

English teacher: I am going to give you a sentence which I want you to correct: 'It was me that broke the window.'
Ambrose: It *wasn't* me that broke the window.

Fatty put a penny in the weighing-machine at the chemist's and stood on the platform for a very long time. In front of his eyes was the chart which told him how much people of different sizes and ages should weigh.

After a while the chemist came over and said, 'Having trouble, sonny?'

'No, I'm just working it out,' Fatty answered.

'Well, did you find out how many pounds overweight you are?'

'I'm not overweight,' said Fatty. 'I'm just five inches too short.'

'Is it very bad luck if a black cat follows you?'

'Well, that depends on whether you're a man or a mouse.'

A doctor was giving a cowboy a physical examination. 'Did you ever have any accidents?' he asked.

'Nope,' said the cowboy.

'Didn't *anything* ever happen to you in a dangerous job like yours?' the doctor said.

'Well, one time a mule kicked me and another time a rattlesnake bit me,' the cowboy answered.

'Don't you call those accidents?' the doctor snapped.

'Heck, no. The varmints did it on purpose.'

Dick's father bought tickets for the football match, but at the last minute he could not go, so Dick's mother decided to see the game in his place. They were rather late in arriving.

'What's the score?' Dick asked the man next to him as he took his seat.

'Nil all,' answered the fan.

'Isn't that wonderful!' said Dick's mother, relieved. 'We haven't missed a thing.'

'Mummy, there's a man here with a parcel for you.'
    'What is it, dear?'
    'He says it's fish, and it's marked C.O.D.'
    'Tell him to take it back, dear. I ordered salmon.'

A tourist went into a field on Farmer Giles' land and began to pick flowers. Suddenly he noticed a bull in the field, and called out: 'Is that bull safe?'

    'Offhand,' Farmer Giles answered, 'I'd say he's a lot safer than you are.'

Grandmother: Richard, what makes your face so red?
Richard: I was running up the street to stop a fight.

Grandmother: That's a very gentlemanly thing to do. Who was fighting?

Richard: Me and another boy.

An old lady reported some time ago that two valuable rings of hers had been stolen. The rings were insured, and the insurance company sent her a cheque for five hundred pounds. Shortly afterwards, the old lady found the rings. She had just forgotten where she had put them. Then she wrote a letter to the insurance company:

'Since I wanted to do the right thing, I decided I couldn't keep both the rings and the money. I am sure you will be happy to know I have given the £500 to the Lord Mayor's Fund.'

Nice old lady: And now, my little man, suppose there were only two pieces of cake left – a large piece and a small one. Which one would you give to your brother?

Willie: Do you mean my big brother or my little one?

Excitable lady: Hello! Police station? Help – come to my house quickly!

Policeman: What seems to be the trouble, madam?

Excitable lady: That dreadful new postman is sitting up in a tree in my front garden, teasing my dog.

An American was visiting Australia.

'Don't you think that bridge is beautiful?' asked the Australian host.

'Well, now,' said the Yank, 'we've got bridges as big as that or bigger at home.'

'What about this park?' asked the Aussie. 'Have you ever seen any like it before?'

'Why, sure,' said the Yank. 'We've got lots of parks bigger than that at home.'

They continued walking till they came to a field. Suddenly they saw a kangaroo hop by. 'Well,' said the American, 'one thing I'll have to admit. Your grasshoppers are a little larger than ours at home.'

Noah was clearing out the Ark after the flood. He lined up the animals, two by two, let down the gangway and said, 'Go forth and multiply.'

The camels marched off. The elephants marched off. So did the ostriches. Then the monkeys and the donkeys got into a terrible row.

'Why are you monkeys trying to get ahead of the donkeys?' Noah demanded.

'You told us to go fourth,' said the monkeys, 'so we didn't want to go fifth.'

Noah finally got everything straightened out, and checked over his list of animals. They had all left except two snakes that were weeping sadly in a corner.

'Didn't you hear me say go forth and multiply?' Noah asked.

'Yes, but we can't,' the snakes answered. 'We're adders.'

The vicar called on the newly arrived family. At one point he tried to get little Johnny into conversation.

'Have I met all your family now?' the vicar asked.

'Everybody except Uncle George,' Johnny replied.

'Which side of the house does he look like?' the vicar continued.

Johnny was a long time answering this one. Finally he said, 'The west side, I think. It has a bay window.'

Mr Smith saw a group of boys clustered round a small dog. His son Johnny was in the group.

'What are you doing?' asked Mr Smith.

'Swapping lies,' said Johnny. 'The chap that tells the biggest lie gets the puppy.'

'Why, when I was your age, I never thought of telling lies,' said Mr Smith.

'Okay, you win, Mr Smith. The dog's yours,' said one of the boys.

Stanley: Dad, how long does it take to get from London to Birmingham?

Father: Two hours.

Stanley: How long from Birmingham to London?

Father: The same. You ought to know that.

Stanley: Well, it's not the same from Easter to Christmas as it is from Christmas to Easter.

A doctor received an urgent phone call.

'Doctor,' said the voice at the other end of the line, 'my wife swallowed my fountain pen two hours ago.'

'Why didn't you phone me sooner?' asked the doctor.

'I've been using my pencil up to now,' replied the husband.

'Mother, I think Grandma needs glasses.'

'Why, son?'

'She's out in the kitchen looking at the washing machine.'

'What's wrong with that?'

'Well, there are two pairs of Father's long pants in it, and Grandma thinks she's seeing a wrestling match on television.'

ABSENT-MINDED PROFESSORS

The absent-minded science teacher brought a parcel into class. 'I caught a frog and a toad yesterday,' he said to his students. 'Now we'll have a test. I want to see if you can tell which is which.'

Then he opened the parcel and took out a ham sandwich and a cheese sandwich. 'My goodness!' he exclaimed. 'I could have sworn I'd just eaten my lunch.'

The absent-minded professor came home and told his wife he felt very ill because he had ridden backwards for two hours on the train.

'Why didn't you ask the person sitting opposite you to change seats with you?' his wife asked.

'I couldn't,' the absent-minded professor said. 'There wasn't anybody sitting opposite me.'

A friend found the absent-minded professor going round and round in a revolving door with a desperate look on his face.

'What's the trouble?' the friend called.

'I can't remember whether I'm on my way in or on my way out.'

After a class the absent-minded professor looked anxiously round the room, then asked one of his students, 'Did you see where I put my coat?'

'You have it on, sir.'

'Thank you very much for telling me. Otherwise I might have gone off without it.'

And then there was the man who put salt on the dog and patted the roast beef.

The absent-minded professor's telephone rang in the middle of the night.

'Is that Central 1212?' the voice at the other end asked.

'No, this is Central twelve-twelve,' the absent-minded professor replied.

'Sorry to have bothered you.'

'Oh, that's quite all right,' said the professor, 'I had to get up anyway to answer the phone.'

The absent-minded professor drove his car into another at a crossroads. His was not damaged, but the stranger's car was crushed.

'Ring me up and tell me how much the repairs cost. I'll pay the bill,' he told the stranger and started to drive away.

'What's your number?'

'It's in the telephone directory,' the professor called back.

'But what's your name?'
'Oh, it's in the telephone directory, too!'

'Oh dear! Oh dear!' moaned the absent-minded professor. He was standing in a bus, holding on to the rail with one hand while his other hand clutched a lot of bundles.

'Is there anything I can do to help you, sir?' asked a sympathetic fellow-passenger.

'Why, yes, there is, if you don't mind,' said the professor. 'Would you please hold on to this rail so that I can get my fare out?'

The absent-minded professor was in his study. The telephone rang, and his assistant said, 'It's a long-distance from London.'

'Quite right,' said the professor and went on reading.

And then there was another professor who put sugar on his head and scratched the pancakes.

When the new term began, the absent-minded professor looked sharply at one of his students. 'Haven't you got a brother who took this course last year?' he asked.

'No, sir,' the student answered. 'I'm just taking it again.'

The professor shook his head. 'Amazing resemblance, though,' he said.

The absent-minded professor got up from the table in the restaurant, took an overcoat from the stand and put it on. Then a man stepped up to him and asked, 'Excuse me, are you John Capper?'

'No,' said the absent-minded professor.

'Well, *I* am,' said the man, 'and that's Capper's coat you're putting on.'

The absent-minded professor moved to a new college. One day he told his landlady that she would simply have to put a full-length mirror in his room.

'You've got a half-length mirror there now,' she said. 'Isn't that large enough?'

'No,' the professor replied. 'You see, I've gone out three times running without my trousers on.'

Three absent-minded professors were talking together in a railway station. They got so interested in what they were saying that they didn't notice the train had pulled in. As the guard shouted 'Take your seats,' they looked up startled and dashed for the platform.

Two of them managed to hop on the train, but the third failed. As he stood sadly watching the train disappear into the distance, a man tried to cheer him up, saying, 'You shouldn't feel too bad. Two out of three made it, and that's a pretty good average.'

The professor shook his head. 'But *they* came to see *me* off.'

Absent-minded professor: If we breathe oxygen in the daytime, what do we breathe at night?
Johnny: Nitrogen.

And then there was the professor who marked examination papers so strictly that he failed three pupils for writing full-stops upside down.

The absent-minded professor said to another professor, 'I'd hardly recognize you. You've changed so much. You've put on a great deal of weight and your hair has turned grey and you don't wear glasses any longer. What has happened to you, Professor Dixon?'

'But I'm not Professor Dixon,' came the answer.

'Remarkable. You've even changed your name.'

Absent-minded professor: I've been feeling run down lately and I've been taking vitamin pills. But they don't seem to help me.
Doctor: Perhaps it's your diet. What do you eat?
Absent-minded professor: Oh, do you have to eat when you take vitamin pills?

COMEBACKS

The teacher had been giving a talk on the importance of milk. When she finished, she asked John to name six things with milk in them.

John thought for a minute, then he said, 'Hot chocolate, ice-cream, rice-pudding – and three cows.'

Mum was the one in our family who made everyone behave. But once she was in hospital for a few days, and Dad had to run the house. At dinner the first night little Sally began to act like a spoilt brat.

'Sally, if you don't behave yourself, you'll have to go up to your room,' Dad said very severely.

Sally didn't look a bit frightened. Instead she just smiled and said to her brother, 'Just listen to Daddy trying to talk like Mum.'

Arithmetic teacher: Billy, if you found five pence in one pocket and ten pence in the other, what would you have?

Billy: Somebody else's trousers.

Arithmetic teacher: Suppose a mother had six children and only five potatoes. How could she give them all their fair share?
Jimmy: Give them mashed potatoes.

A tourist from Manchester stopped at a café in Preston. After a while he began to boast about how many great men had come from Manchester. The café proprietor did not say anything.

Finally the tourist asked, 'Have any big men been born in Preston?'

'No,' said the café proprietor. 'Just little babies.'

Teacher: Now, will someone tell me where elephants are found?
Smart Alec: Elephants are so big they hardly ever get lost.

Question: What do kangaroos have that no other animals have?
Answer: Little kangaroos.

John: What was the name of that chap who used to make his living sticking his right arm down a lion's throat?
Jane: I forget his name, but they call him 'Lefty' now.

Man: What are you eating, sonny?
Boy: An apple.
Man: Better look out for worms.
Boy: When I eat an apple the worms have to look out for themselves.

Tom: You dance very well.
Mabel: I wish I could say the same for you.
Tom: You could if you were as big a fibber as I am.

Bill was playing the violin for his brother. 'Well, how do you like it?' Bill asked.

His brother said, 'You should be on the radio.'

'You mean I'm good enough for that?'

Brother answered, 'No, but then I could turn you off.'

'What did the protoplasm say to the amoeba?'
   'Don't bacilli.'

Once old Jim received a pound too much in his pay packet, but he was careful not to mention it to anyone. During the week, his employer found the mistake and deducted a pound from his wages the following pay-day.

'Hey, I'm a pound short this week,' Jim complained.

'You didn't make a fuss last week when you were paid too much,' his employer said.

'No,' replied the old-timer. 'I can overlook one mistake, but when it happens twice it's time to say something!'

The doctor stood by the bedside, and looked down at the sick man.

'I cannot hide from you the fact that you are very ill,' he said. 'Is there anyone you would like to see?'

'Yes,' replied the patient faintly. 'Another doctor.'

A woman had just about finished inspecting all the trunks in the shop. When there was only one left she said to the assistant, 'I'm not going to buy anything just now. I'm only looking for a friend.'

The weary assistant replied, 'I'd be glad to let you look in this last one if you think she's in it.'

'Did you go to any other doctor before you came to see me?' asked the bad-tempered physician.

'No, Doctor,' replied the patient. 'I went to a chemist.'

'You went to a chemist?' exclaimed the doctor. 'That shows how much sense some people have! You went to a chemist! And what idiotic advice did the chemist give you?'

'He told me to come and see you,' replied the patient.

Son: Dad, will you help me find the lowest common denominator in this problem?

Dad: Good heavens, son, don't tell me that hasn't been found – they were looking for it when I was a kid.

A sergeant was supposed to get some work out of the twenty recruits lined up in front of him. They weren't as energetic as he thought they should be, so he tried using psychology.

'I've a nice, easy job for the laziest man here,' he barked. 'Will the laziest man raise his hand?'

Nineteen hands went up.

'Why didn't you raise your hand?' he asked the twentieth.

'Too much trouble,' drawled the recruit.

Mother: Billy, I was hoping you would be unselfish enough to give your little sister the largest piece of chocolate. Why, even that old hen gives all the best pieces of food to her little chicks, and takes only a tiny piece now and then for herself.

Billy. Sure, Mother. I'd do the same thing if it were worms.

A woman tourist was admiring an Indian's necklace.

'What are those things round your neck?' she asked.

'Alligator teeth,' the Indian replied.

After recovering her composure, the woman said, 'Well, I suppose that they hold the same meaning for you as pearls do for us.'

'Not quite,' he answered. 'Anybody can open an oyster.'

Jim went with his mother to the shop. The greengrocer gave him an apple.

'What do you say to Mr Jones, Jim?' said his mother.

'Peel it, please,' Jim answered.

Nice old lady: And what are *you* going to do when you get as big as your father?

Little boy: Go on a diet.

Landlord: We like it quiet here. Have you any children?

Prospective tenant: No.

Landlord: A piano, radio or gramophone?

P.T.: No.

Landlord: Have you a cat, or a dog, or a parrot that makes a noise?

P.T.: No, but my fountain pen scratches a little.

Tim said to his friend Jim one morning, 'I didn't sleep a wink last night.'

'Nightmares?'

'No, flies,' said Tim sadly.

'Why didn't you dust them off?' asked Jim.

'It was too dark to see whether they were dusty.'

JUST JOKES

A sweet old lady rang up the operator soon after a new telephone was put in her house.

'My telephone cord is too long,' she said. 'I wonder if you can help me out. Just pull it back a little from your end, will you?'

Doctor: What seems to be your trouble?
Patient: After I get up in the morning, I'm always dizzy for half an hour.
Doctor: Then why don't you get up half an hour later?

Joe: Mum, can I have the wishbone?
Mum: Not till you've eaten every bit of your salad.
Joe: But Mum, I want to wish I won't have to eat it.

Kind old gentleman: How do you like going to school, Peter?
Peter: I like going all right, and I like coming home, too. But I can't stand staying there between times.

A man was looking for a job and asked a friend if he knew where to find one.

'Yes,' said the friend. 'I hear they've got a vacancy at the Eagle Repair Shop. Do you want to work there?'

'I'll try anything once,' said the man, 'but I haven't had any experience repairing eagles.'

Mother was telling Father what a bad girl Susie had been. She had had a fight with the boy next door. 'It's all the fault of those terrible Jones children down the street,' Mother concluded. 'Susie learned about biting and hair-pulling from them.'

At this point Susie interrupted, 'That's right. But kicking on the shins was my own idea.'

Aunt Sarah went to the pet shop to buy a dog as a present for her young nephew. 'Are you sure this one will make a good pet?' she asked.

'Certainly, madam,' said the shop-keeper. 'He's very gentle. He'll eat anything, and he's especially fond of children.'

Farmer Giles' son came home from school. He announced that scientists had worked out a way of getting something like milk from peanuts.

'Milk from a peanut!'

'That's what I said,' the boy answered.

'Well,' said his father after a pause. 'I'd like to see what size of milking-stool they use.'

A Boy Scout was hiking along the road with a pack on his back. A battered old jalopy stopped beside him, and the driver offered him a lift. As the jalopy wheezed along, the driver noticed that the Boy Scout still had his pack on.

'Why don't you take that thing off and put it on the back seat?' he asked.

'Your car doesn't seem to be very strong,' the Boy Scout answered. 'I thought I'd do my good deed for today by carrying this extra part of the load myself.'

Little Priscilla's mother thought she was beginning to show off too much. So one night when guests came for dinner, Mother said, 'If Priscilla comes in and tries to attract your attention, don't pay any attention to her. She's supposed to go to bed and stay there.'

Before long Priscilla came downstairs with nothing on but her underwear. She did not say a word as she tiptoed several times round the table. The guests did as they had been told. They pretended not to see her. After a while Priscilla went off to bed, looking surprisingly pleased with herself.

Next morning, Mother heard her say to her brother, 'I rubbed it on and it works. They didn't see me.'

'Rubbed what on?'

'Mother's vanishing cream.'

'Are you any good at figures?' the butcher asked the applicant for the job.

'Yes, sir.'

'Then what would four pounds of beef be at seven pence a pound?'

'Bad.'

'The job's yours!'

'Who shall I ask for?' the customer said.

'My name is Shakespeare, sir.'

'Oh, really? May I ask what your Christian name is?'

'William, sir.'

'Indeed! That is a well-known name.'

'Well, I've been here for ten years, sir, so people ought to be getting to know me now.'

'I'm sorry to have to tell you this,' the time and motion expert said to the pretty typist, 'but I feel bound to put in my report that you waste too much time on your appearance.'

'You go ahead,' she said. 'But I might tell you it hasn't been exactly wasted. I've only been here three months, and I've just got engaged to the managing director.'

Customer: I want some shirts for my husband.

Shop Assistant: Yes, madam. What size collar?

Customer: I don't know off-hand, but if it's any guide I can just get both my hands round his neck.

Arithmetic teacher: Tommy, if you mowed lawns for twenty people and they each paid you fifty pence, what would you get?

Tommy: A new bicycle.

Knock, knock,
Who's there?
Noah.
Noah who?
Noah good place to eat?

Grandpa: I found a horseshoe today. Do you know what that means?

Joe: Perhaps the horse is walking in his stockinged feet.

Knock, knock.
Who's there?
Huron.
Huron who?
Huron time for once.

The mayor had been invited to give a talk at the school assembly. 'I'm going to tell you about taxes,' he announced. 'Can anyone explain what an indirect tax is?'

'Dog licence,' said Tommy.

'Why?' asked the mayor.

'Well, the dog doesn't pay it.'

Tommy's mother sent him to the greengrocer's. After he came home she telephoned the shop and said crossly, 'I ordered three pounds of eating apples and you only sent me two!'

'Madam,' the greengrocer answered, 'my scales are correct. But have you weighed your son?'

Hopeful boy: Good river for fish?
Fisherman: It must be. I can't get any of them to come out.

The class was studying nutrition. When Alec handed in his homework, the teacher said, 'Alec, you were supposed to write a five-page essay about milk, but you only did one page.'

'I know,' Alec answered. 'I was writing about condensed milk.'

Bill: What kind of dog is that?
Will: He's a police dog.
Bill: He doesn't look like one to me.
Will: Of course not. He's in the secret service.

The new doctor's wife was calling on Mrs White. 'I hear your son is a fine football player,' she said. 'What position does he play?'

'Oh,' Mrs White answered, 'I think he's one of the drawbacks.'

Dreamy: I wish I had enough money to buy an elephant.
Practical: Now what do you want an elephant for?
Dreamy: I don't. I just said I wish I had that much money.

Post Office clerk: Here's your fivepenny stamp.
Customer (with arms full of parcels): Must I stick it on myself?
Post Office clerk: No, indeed. On the envelope.

Young Tommy and Willie were watching some men on high scaffolding painting a tall chimney.

'What would you do if you were up there and that thing fell?' Willie asked.

'I would wait until it got almost to the ground and then I would jump.'

A worm received an invitation to a picnic in a field of maize. It went in one ear and out the other.

Mike: Your new overcoat is rather loud.
Dave: It's all right when I put on a muffler.

Grandma: I like to go to bed and get up with the chickens, don't you?
Susie: No, I like to sleep in my own bed.

Instructor at riding academy: What kind of saddle do you want – one with a horn, or one without?

Dude: Without, I think. There doesn't seem to be much traffic round here.

Father (on Coronation Day): Where is Mother, Ted?

Ted: Upstairs, waving her hair.

Father: Goodness! Can't we afford a flag?

Betty: Either the boss takes back what he said, or I walk out.

Hetty: What did he say, then?

Betty: He told me to take a week's notice.

It was the most luxurious greengrocer's he had ever seen, but he could only gasp when he was charged forty pence for a pound of apples.

He gave the girl a fifty pence piece and tottered out of the shop.

'You've forgotten your change, sir,' she said, going after him with ten pence.

'Keep it,' he said weakly. 'On my way in I trod on a grape.'

'My secretary,' said the businessman, 'has been loyal to me for years. I've seen her grow grey-headed in my service.'

'Mine has done more than that. Since she's been with me she's been dark-brown, ash-blonde, and now she's a redhead.'

The lady had no model figure, but the shop assistant did everything she could to help. Her efforts were not appreciated.

'I should like to see just one dress that would fit me,' the lady said in exasperation.

'So would I,' said the shop assistant.

A cranky old lady who lived alone was greatly annoyed because her neighbours forgot to ask her to go on a picnic with them. On the morning of the picnic the neighbours realized their mistake and sent a boy to ask the old lady to come along.

'It's too late now!' she snapped at him. 'I've already prayed for rain!'

Doctor: What's your average weight?
Patient: I don't know.
Doctor: Well, what's the most you ever weighed?
Patient: 180 pounds.
Doctor: All right. What's the least you ever weighed?
Patient: Six pounds eight ounces.

Patient: Doctor, will I be able to read when I get my glasses?
Doctor: Indeed you will.
Patient: Well that's fine. I never knew how to before.

He: Haven't you read the Bible?
She: No I'm waiting for the film.

'Dad, I'm just too tired to study tonight,' said Jimmy.
   'Now, my lad, hard work never killed anyone yet.'
   'So why should I run the risk of being the first?'

Mr and Mrs Jones were writing thank-you letters for presents they had received on their silver wedding anniversary. Suddenly Mr Jones stopped. He looked worried.
   'What's the matter, dear?' asked Mrs Jones.
   'I had it on the tip of my tongue, and now it's gone,' replied Mr Jones.

'Just think hard and it's bound to come back to you,' Mrs Jones said consolingly.

'Thinking won't bring it back. It was a threepenny stamp,' said Mr Jones.

Boy (eating an apple): Gosh! I just swallowed a worm.
Neighbour: Come into the house and I'll give you something for it.
Boy: No, thanks, I'll just let it starve.

'Mum made a bad mistake today and gave Dad some soapflakes instead of cornflakes for breakfast.'
'Was he cross?'
'He foamed at the mouth.'

Young Teddy came home from church looking thoughtful.

'Mum,' he demanded, 'do people really come from dust?'

'In a way, they do.'

'And do they really go back to dust?'

'Well, yes, in a way.'

A little later Teddy came tearing downstairs.

'Mum,' he shouted, 'under my bed there's somebody either coming or going.'

One day a very worried-looking man knocked at Mrs DeVere's door. 'I'm terribly sorry, lady,' he said. 'I've just run over your cat, and I'd like to replace it.'

'Well,' said Mrs DeVere doubtfully, 'I don't mind. But do you think you can catch mice?'

Mother brought little Johnny into the barber's shop, dressed like Hopalong Cassidy and brandishing his toy sixshooter.

'Bang!' he said, climbing on to the chair. 'Bang, bang!'

'I'll be back in half an hour,' the young mother said. 'I've got some shopping to do.'

'I hope the young man doesn't get too restless,' the barber said, worriedly.

'Oh, if he does,' she answered, 'just drop dead for him a few times.'

Mr Jackson: Are you using your mower this afternoon?

Mr Smith: Yes.

Mr Jackson: Fine. Then I can borrow your tennis racket. You won't be needing it.

All his life Mr Jones had spoken with a lisp. At last he decided to take some lessons from a teacher of elocution. A friend met him one day and asked, 'Well, how is it going? Is your teacher any good?'

'Oh yeth,' Jones answered. 'I've learned to thay "Thither Tthuthie ith thewing thirth for tholdierth".'

'That's nice.'

'Yeth, but it ith *tho* hard to bring into the converthathion.'

A farmer consulted the veterinary surgeon about

treatment for his ailing horse. The vet prescribed a powder, and said, 'Roll up a piece of paper into a tube, put the powder in one end, insert the other end into the horse's mouth, and then blow into the tube. That will distribute the powder in the horse's throat.'

Two hours later the farmer was back, choking and with tears streaming from his eyes.

'What's the matter with you?' the vet asked in amazement. 'Didn't you do as I said?'

'Yes,' the farmer spluttered, 'right up to the very last step. Then the horse blew first.'

SHAGGY DOG STORIES

A man sat down in a restaurant and sat his dog in the chair beside him.

'Sorry, sir, but dogs aren't allowed here,' the waiter said.

'But this is a talking dog.'

'If that dog can talk, I'll give you both a free meal,' the waiter replied.

The man turned to the dog and asked, 'What's on top of this building?'

'R-r-r-oof!' the dog growled.

'Now let me ask one,' the waiter said. 'Who is the greatest baseball player who ever lived?'

'R-r-r-roof!' the dog growled.

'I knew all the time he couldn't talk,' said the waiter. 'Out you go.'

On the pavement in front of the restaurant, the dog picked himself up and brushed himself off. He looked up apologetically at his master and asked, 'Should I have said Di Maggio?'

A boy took his dog with him to the film of *Alice in Wonderland*. The dog sat in the seat beside the boy. The usherette came along, noticed the dog, and started to throw it out. But then she saw that the animal seemed to be paying close attention to the picture so she let it stay.

After the show the usherette spoke to the boy. 'It certainly surprised me to see your dog enjoying the show,' she said.

'It surprised me, too,' the boy answered. 'He didn't like the book at all.'

Mary: You know that man who just moved in next door? Well, he's got asparagus growing out of his ears.
Harry: That must be terrible!
Mary: It certainly is. He planted spinach.

Anybody can catch an alligator. This is how you do it. First you get together a telescope, a match-box, a pair of tweezers and a large, very dull book. Then you choose a nice hot day and go to the river bank where alligators live. You sit down, with the telescope, match-box and tweezers beside you, and start to read. Because the day is warm and the book is dull, you soon fall asleep.

Naturally an alligator sees you after a while and comes to investigate. He looks over your shoulder at the book and starts to read it. Because the day is warm and the book is dull, he too falls asleep.

Then you wake up. You take the telescope and look at the alligator through the wrong end. Next, using the tweezers, you pick him up and put him into the match-box.

A magician had a pet parrot that was part of his show. The parrot had seen the tricks so many times that he was very bored. Then the magician got a job entertaining the passengers on an ocean liner. He pulled rabbits out of a hat and then made them disappear. He waved his hands and made a pack of cards vanish into thin air. All the time the parrot sat on his perch and sourly watched the same old show.

But then the boilers in the engine room suddenly exploded and the ship sank. There was nothing left on the ocean but the magician and the parrot sitting at opposite ends of a big plank.

Curiosity finally overcame the parrot. Grudgingly he said, 'All right, I'll buy it. What did you do with it?'

Two frogs sat in a restaurant. One gave the waiter his order, but the other just sat saying nothing. Finally, his

friend asked him why he didn't order. 'I can't,' whispered the frog. 'I have a man in my throat.'

A woman on the Underground noticed that the man sitting opposite her had a pigeon perched on each shoulder. He paid no attention as people crowded on and off at different stations. He just went on reading a newspaper.

Finally the woman got so curious that she spoke to the man. 'Excuse me, sir, but would you mind telling me what those pigeons are doing on your shoulders?'

'I have no idea,' the man answered. 'They just got on at Oxford Circus.'

A man at an auction saw something he wanted very much: it was a parrot. He decided to bid for it. The birds went up and up, but finally he got the bird for £49. Then it suddenly occurred to him that he had not found out the most important thing about his bird. 'Does it talk?' he asked the auctioneer.

The auctioneer grinned. 'Who do you think was bidding against you all the time?'

A man went into a milk bar and ordered a milk shake. He drank it to the last drop, smacking his lips every now and then. At last he said to the man behind the counter, 'That was the best milk shake I ever had. Just to show you how much I appreciate it, I want you to take this for a present.' He reached into his pocket and pulled out a live lobster.

The man did not know exactly what to do, but finally he said, 'Thanks very much. I'll take it home for dinner.'

'Oh, she's already had dinner,' said the customer. 'Take her to the pictures.'

Little Ned was taking his new dog for a walk when a policeman stopped him.

'Has your dog got a licence?' the policeman asked.

'Oh no,' Ned answered. 'He's not old enough to drive.'

Seeing a man and a dog playing chess, a spectator expressed amazement and said, 'That dog would make your fortune in films or in a circus.'

The man was unimpressed and answered, 'I wouldn't say he was as clever as that. I've beaten him four out of the last five games.'

Two pigeons were sitting in their home in the lofty belfry of a church. Suddenly a strange pigeon flew up beside them. The first pigeon whispered to his mate: 'Look at that peculiar pigeon – he's people-toed.'

A man led his horse into one of the largest and poshest department stores in London. He marched up to the lift and asked the operator, 'What floor are leather goods on?'

'Six,' he answered.

The man started to walk into the lift, the horse following.

The lift operator was quite upset about this unusual turn of events and said to the man, 'Hey, you can't do that! Horses aren't allowed in this lift.'

The man turned indignantly and said, 'I have to take him in here. He gets dizzy on the escalator.'

A camel walked into a very fancy Espresso Bar and ordered a banana split. He enjoyed every bite until the waiter handed him the bill, which said '1 banana split, twenty-five pence.'

The camel looked annoyed, but handed over the money.

'Excuse me,' said the waiter, 'but I don't remember ever seeing a camel here before.'

'And you'll never see another one,' said the camel haughtily. 'Not at your prices.'

A television producer heard music in the street in front of his house one day. He looked out and saw an old man, a dog and a horse. The dog was playing an accordion, and the horse sang, while the old man collected pennies from passers-by.

The TV man was so impressed that he got the musicians a job at a thousand pounds a week in his show. But when the day of performance came they did not appear at the studio. Later, the TV man found them again, still playing for street-corner audiences.

'What's the matter with you?' the TV man asked the old fellow who collected the pennies. 'You could be making a thousand pounds a week.'

'No. My conscience hurt me,' the old man answered. 'I don't think it's fair to fool the television public. The truth is, that horse can't sing. The dog's a ventriloquist.'

A man rushed into a doctor's surgery. 'Will you bandage my ear?' he asked. He took a handkerchief from his head and showed the doctor that the ear was bleeding.

'What happened?' the doctor asked.

'I bit myself,' the man answered.

'That's impossible,' the doctor said. 'How in the world could you bite your own ear?'

'I was standing on a chair,' the man replied.

A millionaire lost all his money. With just one fivepenny piece left in his pocket, he decided life was not worth living. He would jump off Waterloo Bridge into the Thames.

On his way to the bridge, he passed a barrow and saw a big red apple that cost exactly five pence.

'No sense in dying hungry,' he said to himself. So he spent his last coin on the apple. He took a good bite and found there was a worm boring a hole inside the apple.

'Good morning,' said the worm. 'My name is Motor. You seem to be very sad. What's worrying you?'

The man told him.

'Well,' said Motor, 'if you promise to take good care of me for the rest of my life, I'll tell you how to make a million pounds.'

The man promised, and soon he had his million. He kept Motor in a beautiful, velvet-lined box. Every day he looked inside to be sure that Motor was all right. And he always asked Motor's advice about what to do in his business. But one day Motor was not in the box. Now the man would have to make up his own mind about what to do. His plans all went wrong, and he lost his million pounds.

Again he had only one fivepenny piece left. He decided life was not worth living. He would jump off Waterloo Bridge. On the way he passed a barrow and saw a big red apple that cost exactly five pence.

'No sense in dying hungry,' he said to himself. So he spent his last coin on the apple. He took a big bite, and as he looked down at the river – out bored Motor.

The new workman opened his lunch-packet and took out two sandwiches. He opened one and peered at it. His face fell. 'Cream cheese and cucumber,' he muttered. The next day he eagerly reached for his lunch, and the same thing happened again. 'More cream cheese and cucumber,' he said. When he was disappointed for the third time running, one of the other workmen asked, 'If you don't like cream cheese and cucumber, why don't you tell your wife to make something else?'

'My wife doesn't make sandwiches for me,' said the new workman. 'I make these sandwiches myself.'

GUESSERS AND HOWLERS

Which horses have their eyes nearest together?
The smallest horses.

What is the hardest thing about learning to ride a bicycle?
The road.

Why do white sheep eat more than black ones?
Because there are more of them in the world.

Why is it useless to send a telegram to Washington today?
Because he is dead.

Why did the jelly roll?
It saw the apple turnover.

Why is an empty matchbox better than all others?
Because it is matchless.

I am something that is lighter than a feather, and yet
   harder to hold. What am I?
Your breath.

Take away my first letter; take away my second letter;
   take away all my letters, and I remain the same. What
   am I?
A postman.

Why does a tall man eat less than a short man?
Because he makes a little go a long way.

Why is tennis such a noisy game?
Because each player raises a racket.

Why do we buy clothes?
Because we can't get them for nothing.

When is a shaggy dog most likely to enter a house?
When the door is open.

I occur once in every minute, twice in every moment,
   but not once in a hundred thousand years. What am
   I?
The letter M.

I am something that no man wants, yet no man wants to lose. What am I?
A bald head.

When do you get like a well-known South American country?
When you are Chile.

Where can everyone always find money when he looks for it?
In the dictionary.

If you saw a counterfeit pound note on the pavement and walked by without picking it up, why should you be arrested?
Because you passed counterfeit money.

If you were invited out to dinner, and found nothing on the table but a beetroot, what would you say?
Well, that beet's all!

If a man smashed a clock, could he be accused of killing time?
Not if the clock struck first.

What is the difference between a man who has eaten a hearty meal and a man who has signed a document?

One is dined and sated, and the other has signed and dated.

What is the difference between a book and a talkative bore?

You can shut up the book.

When is roast beef highest in price?

When it is rarest.

What is the difference between a church bell and a pickpocket?

One peals from the steeple, and the other steals from the people.

When can your coat pocket be empty and yet have something in it?

When it has a hole in it.

When does a man never fail to keep his word?

When no one will take it.

When is a piece of wood like a queen?
When it is made into a ruler.

Where do you have the longest view in the world?
By a roadside where there are telephone poles, because
    there you can see from pole to pole.

When is a sick man a contradiction?
When he is an impatient patient.

What country has a good appetite?
Hungary.

What country does the cook use?
Greece.

Who was the most popular actor in the Bible?
Samson. He brought down the house.

In Biblical times what did people use in order to do
    arithmetic?
The Lord told them to multiply on the face of the
    earth.

When was medicine first mentioned in the Bible?
When the Lord gave Moses two tablets.

When is it socially correct to serve milk in a saucer?
When you give it to a cat.

When was this country put up for sale at a low price?
When King Richard III offered his kingdom for a
   horse.

What is it that is always behind time?
The back of a watch.

What is it that lives in winter, dies in summer, and grows
   with its roots upwards?
An icicle.

What is it that works when it plays, and plays when it is
   working?
A fountain.

What is it that stays hot in a refrigerator?
Mustard.

Why is a healthy boy like the United Kingdom?
Because he has a good constitution.

What is it that goes farther the slower it goes?
Your money.

What has eight feet and can sing?
A quartet.

Who are the best book-keepers?
The people who never return the books you lend them.

Down on our farm we had a hen that laid an egg six
    inches long. Can you beat that?
Yes, with an egg-beater.

How do we know that a dentist is unhappy in his work?
Because he looks down in the mouth.

Why does a person with his eyes closed resemble a bad schoolteacher?
Because he keeps his pupils in darkness.

THAT SETTLES THAT

The following letter to a typewriter repair company got immediate results:

Thmith Typewriter Thervice, Ltd.

16 High Thtreet.

Dear Thirth:

Will you kindly thend a man to my office to repair thith typewriter. Thomebody broke the eth key.

Yourth thincerely,

Thamuel Thimpthon.

Jones: I notice your new neighbour doesn't let his chickens run loose any more. Why is that?

Smith: Well, I hid ten eggs under my forsythia bush the other night. Next day I made sure my neighbour saw me collect the eggs and take them into the house.

Mrs Arbuthnot was always doing good deeds. Early one morning she saw a driverless van slowly rolling down the street towards her. Quick as a flash she jumped into the van and put the brake on. A moment later a very sour-looking man appeared at the window.

'Is this your van?' Mrs Arbuthnot asked sternly.

The man nodded.

'Well, it was rolling down the street and I stopped it.'

'I know,' said the man. 'I was pushing it.'

A man came back to the motor-car dealer from whom he had bought a new car. 'I believe you gave me a guarantee with my car,' he said.

'That's right,' the dealer answered.

'You're supposed to replace anything that breaks?'

'Yes.'

'Fine. I need a new garage door.'

The professor's wife decided to breed chickens as a hobby, but she did not have much luck. Finally someone told her that the Ministry of Agriculture distribute free information about poultry farming, so she wrote this letter:

'Dear Sir:

Every morning I find one or two of my prize chickens lying stiff and cold upon the ground with their legs in the air. Would you be kind enough to tell me what is the matter?'

A few days later she got this reply:

'Dear Madam:

Your chickens are dead.'

Doctor (to patient who had been bitten by a dog): I am sorry to have to tell you that you may have rabies. It could prove fatal.

Patient: Then give me a pencil and paper.

Doctor: For making your will?

Patient: Will, nothing! I'm making a list of people I want to bite.

A disgusted patron in a restaurant called a waiter to his table and pointed to the strange-tasting liquid he had been served.

'What do you call this stuff – coffee or tea?'

'What do you mean, sir?' asked the waiter.

'It tastes like paraffin,' said the irate patron.

'Well, if it tastes like paraffin,' said the waiter, 'it must be coffee. Our tea tastes like turpentine.'

Townsman: Is this a healthy place to live?

Local man: Oh, yes, definitely. When I arrived here I couldn't walk or eat solid food.

Townsman: What was wrong with you?

Local man: Nothing. I was born here.

Frank: Mother, you promised to take me to see the monkeys today.

Mother: Goodness, how can you want to go and see monkeys when dear Grandma is here?

Mum: Dad, you're supposed to take Jimmy to the zoo today.

Dad: Not me! If the zoo wants him, they can come and get him!

Waiter: How did you find your steak, sir?

Sour customer: I looked under a slice of onion and there it was.

Kay: What do you grow in your vegetable patch?

Ray: Tired.

An advertisement for a new soap read:

'Use Lumpo soap. Doesn't lather. Doesn't bubble. Doesn't clean. It's just company in the bath.'

Willie: Mum, you'd better come out. I've just knocked over the ladder at the side of the house.

Mum: I'm busy. Run along now and tell your father.

Willie: He already knows. He's hanging from the roof.

Mother: How did you get Johnny to take his medicine without a sound?

Ingenious father: I shot it into him with a water pistol.

Teacher: What is a skeleton?

Johnny: It's a man with his outsides off and his insides out.

SIMPLE EXPLANATIONS

Billy's teacher asked him to stay after class. 'I think you'd better explain to me why you and your brother handed in exactly the same essay on a trip to the zoo,' she said.

'Same zoo,' Billy answered.

Father: How did that window get broken?
Son: I was cleaning my catapult and it went off.

Teacher: Betty, you tell us where Magna Carta was signed.
Betty: At the bottom.

Arithmetic teacher: If the average car is ten feet long, and if a million cars were placed end to end—
Peter (interrupting): I know the answer. It would be Sunday afternoon on the road to the coast.

Simple Simon: I've lost my dog.
Friend: Why don't you put an advertisement in the paper?
Simple Simon: My dog can't read.

Teacher: Tommy, which is farther away – China or the sun?
Tommy: China.
Teacher: Whatever makes you say that?
Tommy: You can see the sun, but you can't see China.

I was on a train one day when a man farther down the carriage turned to his neighbour and asked: 'Is W-w-w-worthing C-c-c-central the next s-s-s-stop?'

Without answering the question, the second man got up, walked along, and sat down next to me. After a while my curiosity got the better of me, and I asked, 'Why didn't you answer that man's question?'

'D-d-d-do you think I w-w-w-wanted that f-f-f-fellow to m-m-make f-f-f-fun of me?'

Bobby: Dad, what's nuclear fission?
Father (hemming and hawing): Well – I'm afraid I don't really know much about atomic energy.
Bobby (a little later): How do space platforms stay in the air?
Father: Well I don't really know much about space travel either.
Bobby (still later): Dad, how do jets assist a take-off?
Father: It's too complicated to explain.
Bobby: Am I bothering you?
Father: Of course not. You have to ask questions if you want to learn anything.

This happened late one night in a dark street. Two hold-up men jumped out from behind a hedge and grabbed a man who was walking by. He fought like a wildcat, but finally the robbers got him down and searched his pockets. All they could find was five pence.

The robbers stood up, and one of them said in amazement, 'Why on earth did you put up such a fight just for five pence?'

'I thought you were after the three hundred pounds in my shoe.'

Harry: Why does your dog turn round and round before he lies down?

Smart Alec: He's a watchdog, and he has to wind himself up.

Simple Simon was looking at some new cars in London. He seemed to like one streamlined sports car very much. 'Is it a good fast car?' he asked the salesman.

'Fast!' said the salesman. 'If you got in that car now, you'd be in Aberdeen by three o'clock tomorrow morning. Do you want to buy it?'

'I'll think about it,' Simple Simon said, and he went home.

The next day he was back. 'I don't want that car,' he told the salesman. 'All night long I stayed awake thinking, and I couldn't think of a single reason why I'd want to be in Aberdeen at three o'clock in the morning.'

Simple Simon had a piece of rope hanging from a tree outside his window.

'What's that?' asked his friend.

'My weather forecaster,' Simple Simon answered. 'When the rope moves a lot, it's windy. When it's wet, it's raining.'

A man was speeding along the road in his car. A policeman caught him up and made him pull over to the side of the road.

'Why were you going so fast?' asked the copper.

'My brakes are bad and I was hurrying home before I had an accident,' replied the driver.

Farmer (to his wife): What are you doing?
Wife: Knitting up some barbed-wire fence.
Farmer: How on earth can you do that?
Wife: I'm using steel wool.

Mother (to older son): Why is your little brother crying?
Son: Because I won't give him my piece of cake.
Mother: Is his piece gone?
Son: Yes. He cried when I ate it, too.

Mother: Sammy, there were two pieces of pie in the pantry this morning, and now there is only one. How's that?

Sammy: I think because it was so dark in there I didn't see the other piece.

Teacher: Johnny, will you please tell me one use for horse-hide?

Johnny: Well, I suppose it helps to hold the horse together.

I had heard for a long time about an old hermit who was a remarkable weather prophet. Farmers came from miles around to find out from him if there was going to be frost or rain or a dry spell. So, one day, I decided to get his advice myself. But when I questioned him he just shook his head.

'You mean you've lost your power to tell what the weather's going to be tomorrow?' I asked.

This time he nodded. 'Radio's busted,' he explained.

A man walked up to the cashier of a cinema, bought a ticket and went inside. A moment later, he came out, bought another ticket and went in again.

This was repeated several times. Finally, when he bought his sixth ticket, the cashier said, 'May I ask, sir, why you keep buying so many tickets?'

'There's a mad woman inside,' he answered. 'Every time I give her my ticket, she tears it up.'

'My uncle has a truck shaped like a barrel.'

'What does he deliver in it?'

'Cider.'

'That's nothing. My uncle has a truck two inches wide and a hundred feet long.'

'What does *he* deliver?'

'Spaghetti.'

Tommy was finishing his prayers. 'God bless my mother, and my father, and make Montreal the capital of Canada.'

'Why, Tommy!' exclaimed his mother. 'Why did you say that?'

'Because,' explained Tommy, 'I wrote that on my exam-paper.'

Pat: I say, that's a hundred-pound cheque you are writing!

Nat: Yes. Sending it to my sister for her birthday.

Pat: But you haven't signed it.

Nat: No. I don't want her to know who sent it.

Headmaster: Miss Smith, I am proud of your teaching and your class's work. How do you manage to keep on your toes with those very lively children?

Teacher: They put drawing-pins on my chair.

Rubber gloves are things you can put on and then wash your hands without getting them wet.

Neighbour A: Mr Smith's manners have certainly improved.

Neighbour B: Yes, indeed. He has been working in a refinery.

Bright boy: Dad, is your watch going?

Dad: Of course it is.

Bright boy: Then when's it coming back?

'What a terrible bump on your head! What did that?'

'Tomatoes.'

'Heaven! How could tomatoes cause a huge bump like that?'

'They were in a tin.'

Generosity is when somebody gives everybody in the class measles.

An adult is somebody who has stopped growing except round the waist.

The home of a swallow – in the stomach.

Ida: What are you doing, wearing my fur-lined galoshes!

Clare: You wouldn't want me to get your new silver slippers wet, would you?

A caterpillar is a worm with a sweater on.

Pedestrian – a person who can be reached easily by car.

Willie came home from Sunday School and breathlessly called out, 'Mum! Isn't that hair tonic in the yellow bottle on the shelf?'

'No dear,' answered his mother, 'that's glue.'

Willie sighed. 'No wonder I couldn't get my hat off in church.'

Miss Smithers: Who was Captain Kidd?
Archie: He was an acrobat.
Miss Smithers: What do you mean, an acrobat?
Archie: It says in the book that he often sat on his chest.

Johnny's class was having an English lesson, and the teacher called on Johnny to make up a sentence with a direct object.

After some thought, Johnny looked up and said, 'Miss, everybody thinks you are beautiful.'

'Oh, thank you, Johnny,' replied the teacher, 'but what is the direct object?'

'A good report,' said Johnny.

Wally: How do fishermen make their nets, Dad?
Father: It's simple, Wally. They just take a handful of holes, sew them together, and there you are.

Wholesome – the only thing from which you can take the whole and still have some left.

LEG PULLING AND HEAD SCRATCHING

Teacher: Which month has twenty-eight days?
Betsy: They all have.

Smart Alec: Can you spell blind pig?
Ted: B-l-i-n-d p-i-g.
Smart Alec: No, it's b-l-n-d p-g. With two I's he wouldn't be blind.

Question: What goes when the wagon goes, stops when it stops, is of no use, but a wagon can't get along without it?
Answer: A squeak.

Dottie asked her mother this question: 'What has eyes but cannot see, legs but cannot walk and can jump as high as Ben Nevis?'

Her mother thought a long time and then gave up. 'What's the answer?' she asked.

'My doll,' Dottie said. 'She has eyes but cannot see and legs but cannot walk.'

Mother was still puzzled. 'But your doll can't jump as high as Ben Nevis.'

'Ben Nevis can't jump,' Dottie answered.

Smart Alec: If I put three ducks into a crate, what will I have?
Teacher: I don't know. What?
Smart Alec: A box of quackers.

Billy rushed out of the bathroom. 'Oh, Grandma,' he said. 'I saw something running across the floor with no legs!'

'Nonsense,' said Grandma. 'What are you talking about?'

'Water, Grandma.'

Old Farmer Giles was telling some townspeople that they couldn't go any farther. A flood had washed the bridge away.

'I was coming home from town in my old van,' he said, 'when the river rose and carried the bridge away right in front of my eyes.'

'Well, then, how did you get your van across?' the people asked.

'Why, I just sat down on the river bank and thought it over.'

Question: What's the difference between a hill and a pill?

Answer: A hill is hard to get up and a pill is hard to get down.

'Where's your pencil, Maggie?'

'Ain't got one, Miss Jones.'

'How many times have I told you not to say that? Listen: I haven't got one. You haven't got one. We haven't got one. They haven't got one. Now do you understand?'

'Well, where are all the pencils if nobody ain't got none?'

Joan: Is your electric toaster a pop-up?

Fay: No, it's a Red Indian model.

Joan: What's that?

Fay: It sends up smoke signals.

A sheep-farmer was showing a visitor around his farm. 'How many sheep do you think are in that flock?' the farmer asked.

The visitor scratched his head and finally answered, 'I'd say three hundred and nineteen.'

'That's the exact number! How in the world did you guess it?' the farmer exclaimed.

'I didn't guess. I was scientific. I counted the legs and divided by four.'

A motorist had to stop when he found a bridge washed away by a recent storm. A local resident sat near by, gazing blankly into space.

'How deep is this stream?' asked the motorist.

'Dunno,' answered the native.

'Think I can drive through it?'

'Of course.'

With this encouragement the motorist drove head-on into the stream. His car promptly sank out of sight and he himself barely got out alive.

'What do you mean by telling me I could drive through that stream?' he cried furiously. 'It must be at least ten feet deep.'

The native scratched his head wonderingly. 'Can't understand it,' he admitted. 'The water's only up to there on the ducks.'

Mrs Jones opened her refrigerator. To her surprise, she saw a rabbit sitting inside.

'What are you doing there?' she asked.

'What make of refrigerator is this?' he asked in reply.

'It's a Westinghouse.'

'That's what I thought. Well, I'm just westing.'

Pupil: I've added these figures ten times, sir.

Teacher: Good boy.

Pupil: And here are the ten answers.

Farmer: What do you use to treat a pig with a sore throat?

Vet: Oinkment.

Smith: Gosh, how I hate paying taxes!

Jones: As a good citizen you should pay your taxes with a smile.

Smith: That's what I'd like to do. But they insist on money.

Henry: Mum, here's the old-clothes man.

Mum: Say No, Henry. We have plenty of old clothes today.

REAL JOKES ABOUT
REAL PEOPLE

Here is a true story about Mark Twain, who wrote *The Adventures of Tom Sawyer*. After church one morning, he said to the minister, 'That was a wonderful sermon you preached. I have got every word of it in a book at home.'

'I beg your pardon!' said the minister indignantly. 'That's impossible. I wrote the sermon myself only last night.'

Mark Twain insisted he had every word of it at home in a book. To prove it, he sent the minister a copy of a big dictionary.

This is a true story about the great naturalist Charles Darwin. Once two boys decided to play a trick on him. Very carefully they glued together the parts of several insects, including a butterfly's wings, a beetle's head and a grasshopper's legs. Then they took it to the famous man and asked, 'What kind of bug is this?'

'Did it hum when you caught it?' Darwin asked them.

The boys, feeling sure that they had fooled the scientist, said 'Yes!'

'That's what I thought,' Darwin said. 'It's a humbug.'

Not long ago, Greece had a dictator named General George Metaxas. He was both proud and absent-minded, and most people were afraid of him. Once, when he saw a new kind of seaplane, he wanted to pilot it himself. Everything went well until he started to land at an airfield. The young officer with him in the plane was scared, but he said very politely, 'Excuse me, sir, but wouldn't it be better to bring her down on the water?'

'Not a bad idea,' the general answered, and he headed back towards the water.

After the seaplane had taxied to a stop, the general turned to the young man and said, 'It was kind of you to be so tactful, when you saw I was about to make a bad mistake.'

Then he opened the door of the plane and stepped out into the water.

A fortune-teller once prophesied that a close friend of King Louis XI of France would die on a certain day. The friend did die, and the superstitious king was very angry. He thought the fortune-teller had worked some kind of magic that really caused the death. So he decided to have the fortune-teller himself put to death.

'Tell me,' the king said to the man. 'You pretend you are very clever. What is *your* future going to be?'

The fortune-teller suspected what was up. He

answered, 'Your Majesty, I shall die three days before you do.'

After that, King Louis took very good care of the fortune-teller.

When the famous American Daniel Webster was a boy, he often went to school with dirty hands and face. The teacher finally warned him that she would cane him if he did not wash before class the next day.

Daniel paid no attention. The next morning the teacher told him to hold out a hand for inspection. He spat on his hand, rubbed some of the dirt on to his trousers, then showed it – palm up.

The teacher looked and shook her head. 'Daniel, if you can find another hand in the room that's dirtier than this one, I'll let you off without a caning.'

Daniel immediately showed her his other hand.

Sir Walter Raleigh, a descendant of the famous explorer, was on a visit to the United States some years ago and was asked to give a lecture at Yale University. A professor, who had never met Sir Walter, was supposed to pick him up at the railway station. But the professor was held up in a traffic jam. By the time he reached the station, all the passengers but one had left the platform. Rushing up, the professor asked the man anxiously, 'Are you Sir Walter Raleigh?'

The stranger hesitated a moment, then said in a soothing voice, 'Now everything's going to be all right. I'm only Columbus. Just come along quietly with me. We'll find Sir Walter in the station with Queen Elizabeth.'

According to US Government records, there was once a mine owner in Colorado whose name was Amassa Feathers.

During the American Civil War, Abraham Lincoln gave General Hooker an important assignment. The general was determined to make a good impression. He rode round dramatically and gave lots of orders. And to show how busy he was, he sent a report to President Lincoln which gave his address as 'Headquarters in the Saddle.'

Lincoln wasn't much impressed with all this activity. He remarked, 'The trouble with Hooker is that he's got his headquarters where his hindquarters ought to be.'

The Rev W. A. Spooner became famous because he was always getting his words mixed up. A special kind of joke called a 'spoonerism' was named after him. Here are some:

Once the professor wanted to say he had a half-formed wish rising in his breast. This became 'a half-warmed fish rising in my breast'.

'Kinkering congs' came out instead of conquering kings.

At a wedding: 'Is it kisstomary to cuss the bride?'

'Rambling up the scalps' instead of scrambling up the Alps.

Two children named Kate and Sidney became 'Steak and Kidney'.

In a sermon: 'The Lord is a shoving leopard' instead of a loving shepherd.

In a prayer: 'O Lord, in whose hand is the King of Hearts' instead of the heart of kings.

'It's easier for a camel to go through the knee of an idol' instead of through the eye of a needle.

'Cattle ships and bruisers' instead of battleships and cruisers.

'God save the weasel and pop goes the Queen.'

'Fighting a liar' instead of lighting a fire.

'My Canoodian canay' instead of my Canadian canoe.

Trying to say deaf and dumb, he once said 'dem and duff', then corrected himself and made it 'duff and dem'.

'Boil my icicle' instead of oil my bicycle.

Radio interviewers sometimes have Dr Spooner's strange affliction, too. One of them said to Walter Pidgeon, at the end of an interview, 'Thank you, Mr Pleasure. It's been a Pidgeon.'

For a while, when Abraham Lincoln was a young lawyer in Illinois, he was too poor to own a horse. So he walked everywhere. One day a man in a carriage overtook him. Abe waved, signalling for the man to stop. 'Will you be kind enough to take my overcoat into town for me?' he asked the driver of the carriage.

'Certainly,' the man replied. 'But how will you get it again.'

'That will be easy,' Abe said. 'I'll just stay inside it.'

The famous pianist Arthur Rubinstein asked his butler one morning to tell everyone he was not at home that day. He wanted to practise without being disturbed. The telephone rang just as the musician was playing a very fast piece.

'Mr Rubinstein is not in,' the butler announced.

'Nonsense,' said the caller. 'I'm a friend of his. I can hear him playing the piano.'

'No, indeed. You're mistaken,' said the butler. 'I am dusting the keys.'

King Philip of Macedon sent this message to the King of Laconia, a country whose inhabitants were famous for using as few words as possible:

'If I invade your country, I shall lay waste your cities and put your people to the sword.'

The King of Laconia sent this message back to King Philip:

'If.'

A tourist in Washington met Calvin Coolidge taking his usual morning walk. He didn't recognize Mr Coolidge as the man who was President at the time, and he didn't recognize the White House either. The tourist pointed to the White House and asked: 'Who lives there?'

'No one,' Coolidge answered. 'People just come and go.'

DOUBLE-FEATURE
PROGRAMMES

KISS AND TELL
AS THOUSANDS CHEER

*   *   *

DON'T TAKE NO FOR AN ANSWER
ALWAYS SHOOT FIRST

*   *   *

WIFE WANTED
I LOVE TROUBLE

*   *   *

ISLE OF THE DEAD
POINT OF NO RETURN

*   *   *

THE SEA AROUND US
DANGEROUS WHEN WET

LIMERICKS

There once was an elegant Miss
Who said, 'I think skating is bliss.'
　　This no more will she state,
　　For a wheel off her skate
Made her finish up something like this.

　　　*　　　*　　　*

An oyster from Kalamazoo
Confessed he was feeling quite blue.
　　'For,' he said, 'as a rule,
　　When the weather turns cool,
I invariably get in a stew.'

　　　*　　　*　　　*

There was a young lady whose chin
Resembled the point of a pin;
　　So she had it made sharp,
　　And purchased a harp,
And played several tunes with her chin.

　　　*　　　*　　　*

There was a young lady of Norway,
Who casually sat in a doorway;
    When the door squeezed her flat,
    She exclaimed, 'What was that?'
This courageous young lady of Norway.

*   *   *

There was an old man with a beard,
Who said, 'It is just as I feared! –
    Two owls and a hen,
    Four larks and a wren,
Have all built their nests in my beard!'

*   *   *

There once was a man of Calcutta,
Who spoke with a terrible stutter.
    At breakfast he said,
    'Give me b-b-b-bread,
And b-b-b-b-b-b-butter.'

*   *   *

There was a young man from the city,
Who saw what he thought was a kitty.
    To make sure of that
    He gave it a pat.
They buried his clothes – what a pity.

*   *   *

A fly and a flea in a flue
Were imprisoned, so what could they do?
  Said the fly, 'Let us flee!'
  'Let us fly!' said the flea.
So they flew through a flaw in the flue.

S. B. Cunningham
Piccolo Book of Riddles 70p

Q What's red and white, has 22 legs and 2 wings?
A Manchester United.

Q Why is an elephant large, grey and wrinkled?
A Because if he was small, round and white, he'd be an aspirin.

This hilarious collection of riddles, puns and rhyming slang will have you and your friends laughing non-stop!

Michael Holt
Fun with Numbers 50p

Crosswords with numbers ... magic squares ... number patterns ..
join the dots ... missing numbers ... shapes ... curves and lines ..
Hundreds of games and quizzes to prove that numbers are fun.

Tom Robinson
Piccolo Quiz Book 50p
2nd Piccolo Quiz Book 35p

When? Where? Which? Who? What? Here's a great challenge to all Piccolo readers! How much do you know about Sport, History, Words, Music, Peoples, Events, Literature and Rhymes? Here's your chance to find out in these fascinating and informative quizzes.

Norman G. Pulsford
Piccolo Puzzle Books 1–12 50–65p

Riddles, Picture Puzzles, Word Puzzles, Magic Squares, Mazes, Optical Illusions, Quizzes, Limericks – here's a Proper Parade of Positively Perfect Piccolo Puzzles to keep you Pleasantly Perplexed for Hours!

Captain W. E. Johns
Now to the Stars 75p

'Without warning the beast shot forward ... open-mouthed with its back arched, its carapace looking like a row of knives.'

The occupants of the Spacemaster – Professor Brane, 'Tiger' Clinton and his son Rex – journey this time beyond the inner planets of the Solar System, to confront the mystery and deadly danger of alien worlds among the stars.

Isaac Asimov
About Black Holes 75p

Dr Isaac Asimov gives us the facts on this phenomenon in our universe, this swirling mass of matter – or is it antimatter? We now know that a black hole is a star that has totally collapsed, resulting in a gravitational pull so enormous that nothing can escape it. Black holes grow and grow as they suck in more and more matter – science fact, not fiction!

Anthony Greenbank
Camping for Young People 80p

Learn camping – the sensible, practical and safe way – with Anthony Greenbank, author of *Survival for Young People* and *Climbing for Young People*. This complete camping handbook for beginners opens the way for your own discovery of the great outdoors: experimenting in your own garden – choosing equipment – pitching tents – mistakes to watch out for – everything the young camper needs.

Nat Hentoff
This School is Driving Me Crazy 70p

Scatty Sam has problems — how can he get on at school when the teachers expect him to be a 'whizz-kid' just because his father's the headmaster! In his efforts to survive the rough and sometimes violent school, Sam ends up having to oppose his father and face expulsion. He knows a gang of bully-boys are threatening the younger kids ... but will he tell on them?

edited by Biddy Baxter and Rosemary Gill
The Blue Peter Book of Limericks 50p

This collection of limericks is the outcome of a Blue Peter competition. They will really make you laugh, and so will the illustrations.